REBECCA . . .

A BOOK OF
FRAGMENTS AND
DREAMS

UNTHANK
CAMEO

X

In Memory of

REBECCA McMANUS

1993 – 2014

—

First Published in 2017
by Unthank Cameo

www.unthankbooks.com

All Rights Reserved

A CIP record for this book is available
from the British Library. Any resemblance
to persons fictional or real who are living
or dead is purely coincidental.

ISBN 978-1-910061-45-9

Text copyright © Rebecca McManus

Book and Jacket Design by Robot Mascot
www.robotmascot.co.uk

Cover Artwork
The Archer (1879) by Elisabeth Sonrel

Photograph of Rebecca McManus
courtesy of Jack Hobohm

CONTENTS

INTRODUCTION

This is a collection of poetry by Rebecca McManus. Several of the poems have been inspired by her favourite poets including, amongst many others, John Wieners, Raymond Carver, Luke Kennard, Jack Underwood, Amy Lowell, Richard Adlington and Charles Simic.

Rebecca was a talented writer and musician with her whole life ahead of her. Sadly, this was cut short when she was killed by a speeding driver as she waited at a bus stop. She was just twenty-one and weeks away from graduating from the University of East Anglia with a degree in English Literature and Creative Writing.

She had previously been published in Cadaverine Magazine, Ellipsis Magazine, MISO magazine and University of East Anglia anthologies. She was a commended Foyle Young Poet in 2010 and had performed in the West Midlands, Norwich and London, including at the Southbank Centre as part of the Poetry Parnassus in 2012.

In her Twitter profile she described herself as an "Intellectual in waiting, wannabe poet and pun loving beret-ista". She was a kind, loving and generous girl who would do anything for anyone. She was such a gentle soul but had a real zest for life and living. Who knows what she could have achieved? The world could have been her oyster.

She has been described as an exploring and adventurous poet and was thrilled to have had some of her poems published. She dreamt of eventually being able to publish a volume or several of poetry – a dream she sadly never got to see. It makes us extremely proud to be able to do this for her now. This is a collection of her work as it was when she died, therefore several of her poems remain untitled. No doubt she would have re-written others, ever the perfectionist. I hope wherever she is that she is happy with what we have published.

Rebecca's poetry is meant to inspire, for you to look around and celebrate the spirit. "You, I, and the sky" – Rebecca's poems seemed like little adventures, and she loved life's little adventures. If a train journey could take longer so you could see the Olympic Park under construction, then so be it - it meant you were cramming a little bit more living into the day to push out the hum drum and let more light in.

We don't know how many photographs of Rebecca exist. We do know that she smiles in most of them. She was never weary of life – she planned so many things and reached out to experience what she believed in. Although she did not live to see them, she had tickets to see Kate Bush and John Baez in concert in the same week. How many people managed to get tickets for both concerts, I wonder? Rebecca would have known the value of going to those gigs. She would have celebrated the quality and sentiment behind the artists' lyrics in the same way that she had appeared to have collected every record ever produced by Ralph McTell - another artist whose simplistic compositions offered an invitation to reflect on the world around us. And that is what Rebecca did in a way that was filled with gentleness and kindness.

Our beautiful girl was loved by so many and is missed by everyone who knew her – this is a collection of her poems for you to enjoy, we are so proud of her and all that she achieved in her short life. We will love and miss you always Bec x

—Cathy, Gez and Hannah McManus

CLADDAGH

I

If I point my heart out to the world
If I spread my love to all
To reach my favourite someone
To show my heart is free

II

Turn inwards to myself and
The tip pierces my veins and
Sends my love and my lover's
Straight to my true heart

III

Switch hands and switch for life
One person's for all eternity
Locked and chained
Opposite of free,
Love

THE STREET

Peaceful blackout at 1am
No light but my embers
and the stars graffiti above my head
Terraced together in darkness
there is solidarity
A lone taxi prowls the street
Silence is not my enemy

SOME PHILOSOPHY

If no one remembers it, did it actually happen?
If I remember it, surely it did happen?
What is the definition of an event – something that happens?
Who is to say dreams are not real – surely they happen?
I remember dreaming of you, do you remember that too?
Even if you don't, can I pretend you do?
Now I've ascertained it happened, can we live happily ever after?

UNTITLED

Bliss is merely this,
      but I'm in love with this moment
           anyway.

IDEALISM

A room with a harp
A room full of Shakespeare,
A room for contemplation.
I can lie on grass all day
And never get bored,
I can be beautiful if I want to,
Write a book of fragments
And sing echoes of Handel
That I remember.

UNTITLED

To defy Society, I refuse to wear trousers.
To give myself a definable feature, I wear a beret.
To be unlike others, I refuse to follow fashion.
I become penned in by my own follies
until there are more rules in my head than
society ever gave me.

UNTITLED

I want my children to be musical
in all senses of the world.
I want to raise them on travel, folk, and Monteverdi.
I want them to choose their instrument
and stick to it for life.
We'll have lovely sunny days
free from whoever.

UNTITLED

O, for this long and weary March to be over!
A month so dreary that we invent holidays to
amuse ourselves and challenges to keep us awake,
the changeable weather the only thing worth talking about.

Give me the fresh April. Give me free July.
Give me the creeping September, give me back January!

UNTITLED

The sun rises in the odd place
peering in through the branches at me
like a red fiend spreading
its malicious rays of bad luck
on my morning.

UNTITLED

On learning of a death,
I look up at the once blue sky and see that angels have
adorned it with their white draperies.

FUNEREAL

I hate loud shows of emotion,
So I'm going to obscure this with a sense of intellectual
  detachment.
Why do they cry? It's not even you, and it's in a box.
This is our mourning routine; sunset on a Sunday is a nice way
  to begin.
Throughout my whole life, I pictured heaven as a perpetual
  cloud.
Now, thinking of you there, I see my first glimpse of a
beautiful place and realise I've missed the point.
This isn't even real. There's nothing in the box.

AN OUTPOURING OF GRIEF

Notice how the church walls look exactly like
a colour chart.
They obviously couldn't decide which shade
of blue was more consoling.
So they went for all three....
That was the sort of thing they did in the Sixties.
You'll hear all about that from one of the Teresas
later, as she remembers it well.
Eulogy. He was a simple man.
Born anonymously 3/10 on the usual farm.
Emigrated along with the rest 1953.
Married, multiplied, gardened, drank tea.
They decided to frame his
moment of fame, the forklifting prize of 1964,
his quintet of lookalikes making respectful jokes.
It was enough for him to have a life so ordinary.
This from the man so afraid of old age
he refused to be known as "Grandad" ...
If I could have glimpsed the future
I'd have known you'd go first,
but I see you in your garden often enough,
And no doubt I'll see you again.

UNTITLED

We are the stars;
we fly to the moon
gaze down lovingly
at the place that made us

And we see stars
reflected at our stars
the world at night;
constellations of continents.

But look closer
It's not real
There's so much....light
Do we ever see the true darkness that we should?

PROM

The saddest thing about drunken reunions
Is the knowledge that your long-lost friend
Will never remember, and to them, you are
Just another person floating in their past
insignificantly, who they will gradually
allow to be forgotten.

PRETENCE

We've all done it at least once.

Given our name as glamorous Veronica or Marilyn instead of
plain Amy or Louise.
We mean no harm by it – perhaps we don't like the idea of an
intimidating
twenty-something knowing our real name.

But you're supposed to leave it at that.
Tallulah begins and ends in a name, maybe a number.

So what happens when they come to life on the way home?

Celeste plays the flute, has a boyfriend called Rhys, lives in
Kingswinford.
Dervla is a party girl, knows everyone, is definitely going out
tonight.
Meek little Anya draws landscapes in the woods – no, she
doesn't sell them.

I emerge from the bus not myself, but a mixture of whoever I
want to be.
I wish there were more strangers around here so I could keep
up the pretence.
I ignore an acquaintance from around the corner because in
my head we haven't met – yet.

The liberation is breathtaking. A new window has opened in
my head.

Tomorrow I might start a new life.

I SHOULD BE THERE

I sit in my chair in my house.
I look at the dusk.
Well, it's...

     beautiful. But more than that.
It's...

        decadent, yet simple, touching, mellow, and I wish
I was not here, but in some European city where they sing the
opera and madrigals and are surrounded by architecture of the
refined kind, and I should be there, sipping a something and
with a relaxed feeling all in me with great company, cheerful,
positive, just great.

THERE IS A TRAIN

There is a train.

I once found myself abandoned far from my home,
and a beautiful boy told me that
there is a train for me. If I want it.
And I asked myself. "Do I really want to go home?"
I didn't wait for an answer.

Every six months, life starts anew.
Throws something unexpected out.
When it goes wrong,
and you find that you cannot find
where you are,
you must always remember,

There is a train.
Yes, it will take you home.

OCTOBER

October is the 5 o'clock of the year.

Before the anticipatory 8 o'clock eventide of November,
the party that is December's 10 o'clock comes the lull:

We are tired but do not acknowledge it,
would secretly like the year to be out and a fresh one in,
we are dragged down with the mundane dinner of slushy
   leaves and the winter coat debate.

THE ELEMENTS

You hold the cigarette of your life
 up to your face
 and the ashes blow with the wind around you.

The spark tries and fails to warm you, but it was a nice
    gesture.
Howling winds and sugary rain
beat us in a blanket of mild chagrin.
We pace the good tarmac.

All around me is music but as I walk higher and further the
elements surround me and cut me off from where I want to be.
Tonight I feel alone.

DISSATISFACTION

Life moves too slowly for you. Too fast as well.
You hate change but you wish life was different.
We all reminisce; we all wish our lives away.

Life:
waking dissatisfaction.
walking contradiction.
stalking penetration.
sulking commiseration.
hulking commendation.
King of Conversation.

THE END OF THINGS

The sun burns on terracotta
and slowly cooks the air
in a gentle manner.

Half-tears muster up the courage to
think about appearing.

Once, things were better, were they not?

But there is always
the stain on the cloth,
chip in the screen,
blemish in the gemstone
imperfection in the fabric of life.

What can I do?
I throw my hands up and
bear this as romantically as possible.

What happened?
Blame the beautiful evening
that could have been.

Words sting me to the heart,
a warm icicle melting.

PROMISE

These clouds are magical tonight.

I love this time of year. The calendar tells me that
    Midsummer Day is
next Thursday; I tell myself that it is tonight. Who can put a
    date on midsummer?
Next Thursday it could be a rainy March, and, in all
    likelihood, I will be wearing tights.

Take me to a field, let me gaze at the
wispy thoughts across the blue page above my head. If you
let your mind wander far enough, it says, "Promise" in the
west. I am not concerned with the promises of what I will do
    tomorrow.
Just what it will bring.

Make me a twilight daisy-chain
and hope that magpies stay far away from this place.
I never want to leave. When I die, do you think I will come
    back here?

Soon you will take me down the dusty road home. We are
    weary with the
heat that has not yet left the path. Our shadows stretch
behind and cling to the edge of the horizon, refusing to leave.

But then you help me over the stile.

Civilisation appears.
The air is nudging me, because it knows something wants to
   happen. Tarmac and newspaper roll by and I realise with a
   sigh that the moment is gone.

You turn away; you'll see me tomorrow, like you always do.

REALITY

Why do you torture yourself with things that will not happen?

The cruel glee on the face of fate
as you sink
to your knees and howl at the sky,
Greek tragic, navy storm clouds.
Maritime climate.

For all the times you've pictured the perfect life,
there are a thousand sorrows.

Be realistic. Nothing interesting happens. Don't glorify your
mundane life by making it tragic when all you do is sit
around and wait for something to come along and drag you
into a far-fetched romance.

ON CHANGE

... and every day there is a moment when we will think of
absent friends and times that used to be.

Pause; subdue your laughter. For there was once a life you
used to live that is now less than a dream.

Cherish the present – love everyone – never forget your old
friends old thoughts and maybe old habits –
Hark! The clock ticks, does it not? The end of this moment is
near and I fear I shall soon go –

How will you remember a faded friend ...?

MEMORIES

Magical magical magical nights of my life when everything is beautiful beautiful beautiful. Put a star on your calendar, try to remember how you felt (but don't reminisce too often or you'll never let go.)

Remember how you danced. Remember why you laughed. Remember what he said. Remember who you loved.

Now stop.

You know you've gone too far when you close your eyes and try to hear the music you'd forgotten they played. Stop before you wish you could die and replay the best bits of your life over and over again.

Magical magical magical ...

ORGANIST

I sit at the majestic instrument and try to feel
in control. I play
an Elegie; so simple on such a complex
instrument.

Digress –
the nauseous feeling of nervous pain as I ignite the insides,
the decision of knowing which stops will pull my
heart-strings.
the rough yet smooth pedals that I can't quite co-ordinate.
One day I'll know
the full power, and so will someone else.
I won't see their face and they won't see mine;
maybe they are already here.
I'll never know
whether it is a vast open space

behind me

or not

the Organist.

SIBYL

A cold night of snow
Sibyl beholds the moon;
Waxing crescent.
She thinks:
"People are like waxing crescents.
Show off a little slither,
Obscure the rest from view."

SUN

Sometimes, I feel like I go round in circles.

As I forced myself to wade through the thick, icy air,
I saw my queendom ablaze with a
perfect Autumnal sunrise.

I thought it was beautiful,
but it came back to spite me.

By midday, I was cruelly blinded by
the searing sunlight,
seeping in through my squinted eyes.

And in the evening,
I curled up in my freezing house
as the light
drained from everything.

Each day, I am betrayed by the Commander, my sun.

HALF-MOON

This is my view.
Half-moon
Rising
Nearly
Eventually
Gradually
It'll dawn on me

It's never coming up.

Why is it there
Who put it there
When did it come
Was it when
My view turned
Bright
Light

It stays half-moon.
Sometimes, we look way too much into these things...

The stars are out for once
They're different
Missing
Twilight
Not the same.

CHARACTERS

The Wanderer

Those who wander
have sinned, we
heard. This Peregrine
                    of the modern
                    world never rests,
                    but not for
                                        conscience – just for
                                        want of something
                                        other to do.
                    He runs, but
                    he doesn't know
                    what from. Perhaps
he did know,
but did he
forget? Is that
                    why he travels,
                    the open road
                    his home, as
                                        he wanders the
                                        world?

THE MESSENGER

Admirable, really, that courage and perseverance for the safe

delivery of a message not his own. The messenger is killed

so often these days, in conversation, it is a wonder that he

still exists. Did he run with winged feet 'round the world?

Did he carry your words at his breast? He flies through

the air, unseen, quicker than Hermes, wherever you want in

five seconds. Ask the messenger what his thoughts are in the

matter. Maybe then he will never lose interest, or post.

THE OBSERVER

He likened himself to a star of the north
gazing down
(a star of the south on lazy days,
gazing up).

Aldebaran, perhaps.
The follower. Chief watcher.

There is history, and there are
history's narrators. The observers.
Those who refuse to get involved.

He sits at his globe and gazes with
wide eyes that have seen it all,
yet seen nothing.

For once, he is the protagonist of his own brief story.

As for me? Never mind that.

OF THE NIGHT

It's horrifically amusing
when you discover
that absolutely nothing is as it seems...

Laugh in shock
as several things
dawn on you at once:

she has a secret – he's in love with that girl – as for him; he
  always knows more than he lets on

Forget the daylight hour
where all is conventional
and people tell jokes
of no relevance

Give me the dark night
The true nature of people
The delicious sense of rebellious togetherness
Against an uncertain future
with a more uncertain past
in the most uncertain present

PEACE

Because you blink,

and eight months have gone by.

Go back to when you were lying there in the arms of all,
that multitude of unattainable arms,
and it was cold outside but beautiful nonetheless.

I hate to remember such a
perfect moment
because peace should remain peaceful,

undisturbed forever.

AN APOLOGY

He chanted, chanted, chanted.

Maybe he's right. I should spend my days
making the house. House making.
Making a house a home. Home making.
Keeping it like that. Housekeeping.
While we're on the subject, what does Excalibur mean to
    you?

Everything.
Excalibur means everything to me.
I'm so sorry, I wish I could concentrate, but that floorboard is
    creaking
and it bothers me. Persistently.

All around me there are white things hanging on white
    radiators.
Also, it snowed all day long.
My point being that I can't tell
if it is a reflection of myself,
or a mockery of what I will become.

Have I strayed so far from the flock?
I hate to say it but my life is much better since I left.
The confession that I will not make stares back at me. I am
    wrong.

Films are so immoral these days, don't you think?
Escapism is one thing. Yes, it is one thing, but could it be
    many things?
This is many people's house. Keep your bit tidy if you will.

My mind drifts when the floorboard creaks. I'm sorry.

I am an anomaly in my age group. So I'm told.
But I keep adapting to my surroundings
Until I've told so many lies
I can't remember
Who I am to each person I know
What version of me they get
And whether I will go to Hell for any of this

THE MASS MARRIAGE

Life became unbearable
A short while ago,
So we devised a solution
To cheer us up:

Let's be happy
Let's massively marry
The air is cold, but
That horizon is pink.

Tonight we aren't soldiers,
Or anything unpleasant,
We are grooms and the best of men,
And our whole life is now.

Soon enough we'll be encircling
The waist of a beautiful woman,
Ours for an eternity
Or a day, or both.

Tomorrow will never be forgotten
By history, but only we remember
The mass marriage.
Our night. Let it remain so.

We'll be happy.
We'll massively marry.

HAPPY 20TH MARCH.

One day of the calendar becomes the one you choose
to read the synopsis of your life so far,
note where you have been
and where you are going.

You think you've barely begun to be anything,
but your contemporaries are
ending their plays at seven scenes and
closing their eyes for forever because
they've seen all they need to see
and will keep all they need to,
forever.
They are wrong.

I wish I could write
something more than a fragment.
I wish I had invented the word 'fragment'.
I wish I was making a
witty, observant, legitimate point and
 I wish I could handle sarcasm.
Even idealism has me thrown,
because surely to know your ideal,
you've denied some ruthless facts?

Well I was going to make a
relevant remark about rainbows,
but it's getting late so
I'll leave it for another day.

I'll look at this, my maiden speech,
in several years' time, and find
things that were never really there,
and are certainly not here now.

THE LOVERS

1

Breathe, Love, Breathe.

How you circle her in your arms.
How she throws herself into them.
Thick curls entwine. Breathless laughter.

I am more interested in minesweeper than you. And you.
I am - sweep my bones up and be mine:
I would be if I'd been back on time.

You, a colossal Roman plinth;
She, a statue with adoring eyes upon it;
I, the tourist.

Not upset, just mildly melancholic.
Everyone here thinks this is strange, but
We simply gaze at the lovers.

I do apologize if my mirth is overflowing.
Go back to your picture of happiness.
I've never seen her smile so wide.

When I was thine for two minutes...
But we don't remember that.
Leave me, let me lie, drift and pine for you.

2

Sigh, now. Sigh.

There was a time when I cared.
More an idle curiosity than true feeling.
I'm still bemused, but not unpleasantly.

It's far too coincidental.
Stop talking, you'll be fine. We'll all be fine.
Too much heartbreak in one sentence.

I don't see her around anymore,

Do you, I wonder? Come hither,
We can pine together. Your loss.

Not my gain. Once again, the time
Is against us. Not that we are us.
I was never thine. Was she?

Sometimes I think it an elaborate lie
That two curls could entwine and then
Retreat within a month or less.

Let it lie, now, let it lie.
We'll all secretly remember this as a half-dream,
But none so vividly as I.

COINCIDENCE

The jarring, shocking, mocking parallels in my life
that make me want to drop to my knees
in a nondescript unemployed midlands town,
yes,
drop the shopping and cry,
give up,
sell my soul to whoever's asking.

At this point I will realise that

Life is not real, and never has been,

Or,

That however hard I try,
I cannot faint at will and
I need to pick my shopping and myself up before they build a
    road over me.

I CAN'T FIND THE WORD

Paper tears internally
The enemy holds the word down in your throat,
Throws ropes around your tongue to torture you...

You cannot rest until you know it
Employ your hands to do the work instead,
Rip through pages until it
leaps out and frees you...

Say it.

CLASSIC

I too was a young and thrusting student,
Until I awoke one day and saw
that the one I lay next to
utterly repulsed me.

Now, Cicero is my man,
those reams of pages of levelled argument
comfortably substituting for daily disputes over dinner.

I'm not Medea.
I'm not Medea.
Living in the past is terrific,
and yes, it's enough for me
(though I'm unsure if the dog feels the same).

I just have to be careful
    I don't wake up one day and realise
        I've been trapped in a cupboard
            for 103 years, alone...

HOW WOULD YOU LIKE TO SPEND YOUR JULY?

Well perhaps this is a disclosure for a more eloquent time,
but that is exactly the problem.
Time is my enemy. Time is my bad luck.
I remembered this and more as I sat
staring at a small red light
in an unusually long gap
between dance performances.

The surrounding blackness
embraced the audience,
bound us together
for a few short moments,
unable to let go of this most maternal of instincts.

This monster mother of darkness
knows how alone we are,
tried to help,
        tried never to leave.

But it did, and there was a dance, and I will never sit on that
    seat again,
like I will never know how a character can change so much.

FIRST OF OCTOBER

Unseasonal happiness strolling around heaven.
If you were here would that be better or worse?
Harp plays, sun bathes, trees wave...
If they could
I must have died, because this is too good for a sinner

UNTITLED

The moon is my flower, stand by me,
Stride about because you own this lake.
"What was the promise that you made"
Not never, not now.
You're content, so I am too.
Lakeside strolls through Dante's Inferno.

EXPECTATIONS....

What I wanted to happen
What could have happened
What might have happened
What should have happened
What would have happened
What I thought would happen
What I expect to happen

UNTITLED

Darkness came when the clocks went back and you revealed
     your
dark side to me.
The moment I read those words I knew they were true
of me, and I will never know if it was you.
And I should have said so much more, so where are the
words I didn't say?
All this happened, and the heaven illusion faded.

UNTITLED

If I was painter, I could catch the red haze above the lake,
in-between the two halves of hazy beautiful blue, the
    silhouettes of
trees the frame.
If I was a musician, I could play the way the brightness
melts into the horizon along with the deep, threatening wood.
But I am a writer, and before this sweet moment leaves
me for good I must somehow notate the divine beauty of
    what
I see, now as I look out of my window this November sunset.
Look at your sunset. Alone. Listen to beautiful music
And....live.

UNTITLED

The closest thing to peace I have found here;
a tranquil morning, mist still rolling. The sun is up
and the moon hangs like a forgotten Christmas
decoration in the sky. I'm not even alone, for there
is a face over there, not content with admiring from
a distance like I, but no, she has pushed her face as
far out the window as possible, bearing the full force of the
crisp morning air. The first frost.

UNTITLED

Number 9 bus home
(It's always the 9, just like it's always a Thursday)
and I'm smiling.

Sixteen, an optimist, an idealist,
full of what might be a hint of love

I don't care it's muggy late summer,
it's rush hour, there are Primark bags everywhere
wilting in the heat and that damp, cheap cardboard smell

But I have a coffee cup.
A paper coffee cup, tiny, Starbucks expresso size, with
Words inside that are all I've ever wanted to see,
Addressed to me,
From him.

I keep my coffee cup
And wonder where my happy expectations went.

UNTITLED

It was the carpet, darkened by twenty odd children growing
    up
It was the dark entry, echoing footsteps and fingerprints on
    Victorian bricks
It was the front bedroom perfect for games
It was the kitchen, friendly in its stark white decor and bleak
    lights
It was the scratched and stained table in the window
It was the garden, the wall to jump from and the constantly
    ruined flowers
It was the one armchair completely out of bounds
It was the curved mirror on a plate hanging oddly on the wall.

THINGS THAT MAKE ME SMILE

Waking up from a wonderful dream believing it's true
Waking up from a nightmare knowing it wasn't
A well-timed compliment from my favourite person
When things go exactly as I hoped they would
(Little moments when I realise I am loved)
Friends who, unasked, did something for me.
Bright early mornings, alone with my thoughts
Reading old diaries and remembering my (youth) naive
teenage years
(Finding someone who knows completely what I am
Ranting to friends about everything that's annoyed me.

UNTITLED

Swans can't fly.
Given the choice would you exchange
beauty for wings?
They skim the lake like chariots, heads aloft, keeping dignity
whilst the ugly seagulls rise and fall above them,
screaming with the burden of flight.

NOT REAL

Tricolour barges rest in the aching sunlight
Silently creaking with the burden of regrets
Banished for now, with those clouds, made of sonnets

Leaf skeletons flutter in like gold filigree
Twisted like paper roses tossed away
By pylon giants who walk hand in hand
But this was not real
Now the dangerous clouds of last night's dream
Bear down on this cluttered road

Unfeeling mountains refusing to give advice
Showing their darkness as futures are decided
With rain, the angry rain

For the next month it will rain sporadically
like tears that fall involuntarily far too late
with a childish hateful delight

THINGS LEFT UNSAID

(he)	I want to see you again
(she)	Take my number
(he)	Let's go for a drink tonight
(she)	Today was the best day of my life
(he)	Are you as happy as I am?
(she)	You could be my whole future
(he)	I don't deserve you
(both)	I love you
(she)	I lied
(he)	I forgive you
(she)	Things have changed now
(he)	Let's talk about this
(she)	I don't want you to go
(he)	I miss you
(she)	I want to see you again.

A ROMANCE, PART 1 [DARKER]

A theatrical romance
with a Romantic touch –
dressed in black,
I with my dark mask,
you in funereal cashmere.

A riverside walk through the shadows
with melancholic smiles
and fingers entwining
(secretly)
like tree roots
(underground)

Give me your answer
along with your best wishes
by the end of the week,
and until then,
there are
fervent looks,
(hands held),
long hugs full of longing
and heartbeats.

A ROMANCE, PART 2 [CROMER]

You and I, on the seafront, on the edge of England.

We are the only people here
and as I face the sea,
I will believe the land is gone too
especially if you tell me.

I sit with you in the present
Ahead is our unknowable future,
blurry visions on a horizon full of promise, or bleak despair
behind are the faded glories of yesterday,
unchanging yet painfully crumbling,
being forgotten.

The sky is divided
ideal to the left,
pure storm to the right,
and through the middle
shoots a perfect rainbow
from the sky that cannot decide.

If a bird flies away, repeatedly,
would it have anything to leave behind?
And would it ever come back to Cromer?

A ROMANCE, PART 3 [LIGHTER]

We lie together,
like we did before
You lie to me
I pretend you don't
And to the others we're the happy couple
we never said we were.

From my mouth you took kisses and
"I promise to forget you"
But how can I keep it since you took it from me?

And now a storm from the south springs up,
floods my room with pathetic fallacy.
I pretend it's your tears
but really it's my own
weeping for your sins.

And I can listen to the tempest, wishing you in it,
Play a lacrimosa, remembering the days I met you,
Smoke a pensive cigarette, hoping you'll walk past,
But I will always want to be
with you,
entwining hands,
on the seafront,
lying in pretence
with you,
until I forget you,
or the end.

AUTUMN DISILLUSIONS

Early morning,
the grey sky doesn't glitter.
I sit here and
think about all the men I have sat here with,
including the one beside me.
You were my favourite.

Afternoon,
the yellowing sky is hazy.
I sit here and
look at the hole-punched clouds,
wondering who is being blessed with a glittering
revelation.
I should be outside.

Dusk,
the purple sky still doesn't glitter.
I sit here and
lament that I am buying a semi at such a youthful
age.
Lights jump on elsewhere and ignore me.
The lake glimmers, perhaps.

Days like today
are not what I live for, or what I die for.
Unseasonable weather usually brings
unseasonable happiness,
but today is just missing.

Soon after sunset,
never mind.
I just saw the blue sky glitter

OPTIMISM

He was just so upbeat all the time,
they called him a cloud of happiness.
His only concern was his grave allergy to ice cubes,
so this clever cloud exchanged them for sweets,
which he exchanged for bottle tops, to bake with.
"The glimmering chocolate cake", thought this crazy cloud.
His one daydream: confectionery that dazzled, literally.
Once, he woke up to discover "bad luck"
written in the hills around him, in bottle tops.
It was a clear, cloudless day.

OBSERVE, YOU WILL FIND HOPE

Go looking for answers
    in absurd places
        and you will find
           absurd things
So look in normal places, and find normal things.

Happy lovers rushing down a false-lit path
"Keep walking!"
A forgiven enemy wandering like the minstrel he'll never be
An unknown figure running from unknown things
Two insignificants.
Indescribable howling of despair, or perhaps excitement
A fire glowing distant/constant
and a friendly stranger who berates you for your rudeness.

Don't you see now?
Doesn't it all make sense now?

POST-

When
music is
played above
lovers it gives them
strength, and when one
edge from a triangle disappears,
it becomes an angular crescent, points
touching, yet running. But this devastating
crescendo was beautifully killing us like ohimes
and petit-morts and it must go on for you and I were
each on a different line, always going the opposite way,
until we were deafeningly together, yet so far apart.

GLASS

This sorrowful face
I took as my own,
as did they who once walked past me,
my congregation.

I used to project
faces on faces,
woe upon woe
Or I brightened
gave an illusion of warmth
with glimmers of
the yellow hope or red passion
so denied to them.

Now my choir of empty promises,
my worshippers of stone
are gone.

I want to inspire fear into rebels
who break in for an ironically bad time,
but they don't even see me.
One day may even smash through me.
Until that day
I am fixed in my devoted sadness,
forever cold,
forever stained.

HORIZON

What does the sky do?
Not kiss the trees, no –
it meets with them,
comfortably, carefully,
interlocks gently,
harmonious together, abstract
companions of nature

LIE

And I suddenly noticed
that I can't tell the difference between asleep and awake,
because people appear in my head
as they do in my life.

And I also noticed
that I keep lying to myself
despite being faithful to others.

And although I've forgotten you,
your sad, "There's something I'm not telling you" face
follows me around, and I can't tell
if you are here, lying to me, or there, telling the truth,

And are they merely the same thing?

Because what is a dream if not a lie?

MEMORIAL

All tragedies are just accidents, that happened.

Where's Romeo now? Over there, a girl mouthed something *colourful*, and he took it to mean *I love you*. And so began a year of shyness and agony, until he disappeared. His memorial stone shows us how long we have left. He's been gone a long time. We think he's in the lake.

Remember when we said that everything would change, and it did? There's a paranoid performer to my left who had his suspicions confirmed when he once tried to open a locked door. "Never mind; we can exeunt through this wardrobe." Why? "She asks too many questions," he added conspiratorially.

I remember when I was awake. But that drink was strong, a little too strong, if you ask me, and now I am stuck here again, a geranium, an unreliable, unrealistic, unobtainable voice with a blanket of trouble ready to smother me if I don't find it by next Tuesday.

Because all tragedies are just accidents, that happen

EVERY MONDAY MORNING

I walk down this path of concrete memories

the melting snow framing my walk

like a ripped photograph

The snow, the ominous snow

TAKE MY HAND

fingers stuffed with clouds lined up in a row
like a steam train's breath
or corn, crudely tied

next to the giant sheep
that the villagers of this plain worship,

children skipping down the life lines
of their dust bowl

the sun forever the colour of memory

SHADOW

Notice how the night is when you are bravest
because your shadow got so tall it became you

Notice how the night is when you are darkest
because your shadow got so tall it became you

Notice how the night is when you are most afraid
because your shadow got so tall it surrounded you

Notice how the night is when you are most pure
because your shadow got so tall it left you

VICTORIA EMBANKMENT GARDENS, 30TH MAY

To the stranger I fell in love with:
    I hope you enjoyed your lunch and your roll-up.
    Carry on walking into the sun.
To the one who abandoned their wallet and phone:
    I hope you succeeded with your new identity.
    And that your new loved ones miss you more than the old.
To the five mothers and babes on my right:
    I hope your home lives are this simple and happy.
    Grow up in safe ignorance.

ONE NIGHT STAND

The absolute loss of innocence
    Discarded like an old bus ticket

The white dress you barely remember shedding
    Lies where you flung it for good

Alcohol

FOREVER YOURS, THE LAKE

Lead me on, to the woods. Our own selva oscura.

My sight is blurred
    from what you gave me in a hollow tree
    from what I gave you in our hollow tree
(where a tramp lives?
    or where kids go to smoke?)

It's nice and twilight, I say,
I follow you through imaginary fields
and stumble on roots

You take me to hell, or a jagged sunrise
    or are we looking for the real world
    is that why you don't look back:
    to save me?

Walking so far we'll fall off the edge soon
won't we?

BONFIRE

The embers chatter silently
    like a city destroyed by war
And we scatter them across their broken country,
    dust and ashes.

The bonfire dies, the drunk man cries,
    we leave together knowing
That we did no harm, but did no good.

DO NOT TAKE ANY RISKS

Do not take any risks.
Live life in the safety of the carriage,
mind the gaps
of society,
those who fell through the cracks,
where did they end up?
Continue to ignore the blind beggar
and keep calm and carry on,
and Do not take any risks.
Mind the gaps between sentences
that you dare not acknowledge,
Mind the gaps in your life
and fill them with money.
But this could still be Merry England,
with liquorice Rizlas and pork scratchings,
the McDonalds philosophers who ask,
"What is the colour of mutiny?"
and the Shakespearean Fool who lies slumped at the bar.
Tricycles that can't fly sit on council estate balconies
Some poor boy stands around all day, waiting for a riot to
happen
People walk around with umbrellas when it's not even
raining
This is what England is
Life is more than just waiting to die
It's the dreadful shudder of a passing train
It's the thought of dancing in the rain
It's the knowledge of the whole world's pain

But still they say:
Do not take any risks.
Do not gamble,
Do not invent,
Do not trust your terrible instincts
And do not dream.

A GUILTY TITLE

(read with a struggle)

How many times
have I tried
to say sorry

Venice
is crushing me
and my conscience

And yours

Comments are closed

STILL

Rented. Furnished.
Let these things be mine.
Let me use this appliance like I own it.
Let me force my character on this room.
Don't let the house have the power.

Now there's nothing beautiful about a drab ten-year-old semi
   in suburbia.
Shaky doors.
Creaky beds.
Cold kitchens.
Student living.

"Your room is really just a long letter to yourself."
I've stopped my clock and now it's only a decoration.
Useless.

I have nothing to write about except food and silence.
I fear I'll always be too young to say anything significant,
and I'll always be here,
like the stagnant lake.

DECISIONS

I sat there
on the tip of a crescent moon
and a pond rippled,
like a person changing their mind

POT OF GOLD

I saw you
when you first found that pot of gold.
I saw you laugh at the legends;
     climb back up the rainbow
          until you were high above me
     take golden apples for yourself
     let everything you touched
          make you glitter inside.

You said,
"It's not gold but it's as good as".
You told me of the gold rush,
     right to the heart,
     the heart of gold.

Diamonds trickle down your face.
Cling.
     Clang.
          Trinkets for me.
Metallic taste in my mouth.

I no longer have you,
     I have my pot of gold.

GRANNY

"If the Virgin Mary appears,
make sure you wave"

I have twenty-one grandchildren
and I never told one of them this.
Look at them,
ten-year age gaps tightened by blood,
mine, I suppose.
I have the baby, freshly christened,
because I know what to do by now.

The sun will start to go down soon,
I think.
The children frolic in a
perfect picture of a tranquil afternoon.
They can forget
the cancer and the divorce and the jail sentence
but I won't.

The sleeping one knows nothing but my frail arm,
rocking a-bye.

ALIGHT

This life of mine became too full to know
The truth or lies of anything at all
If I could only know I would not fall
For lies, for love, for you and I could show
My reason, mercy, sympathy and woe
For you, not I, those times when I would call
You over, listen to those stories, tall
Untruths and you should know I would not go.
Remember when we found that lonely place
Unseen by daylight, glowing with the night
Whose smoke obscured and brightened up your face;
The last I saw before your timely flight
From fire and wasteland leaving just a trace
Of vapour, mist and dreams that set alight.

INK

yes
you are a star.

well, you could be brighter
you're getting weaker.

(and weaker.)
still

"black weather"
"blotting out the stars"

the biggest ink-pen.
thunder clouds spreading

rain seeping in everywhere
obscuring all the words

standing still with no umbrella
saturated, disintegrating

you are no longer something to see
just something that was once seen

THE LINE

I'd rather find the will to live than sit
Here with my aging poker darling. "Try
To find yourself a beauty that can fly" –
I think they mean a bird, well that's bullshit.
Maybe I should dream one for a bit
And see if that goes well. Well somehow I
Can't see how that would work, they don't have my
'Best interests' in their hearts it seems. I lit
A candle just to watch the trail of smoke
And found myself inside a glass of wine
I ate a truffle but it made me choke
My faded wife reminded me she's mine.
I'd love to dance with all the other folk
But that all ended when I crossed the line.

FIRE STATION, 12 A.M.

Nothing strange about a midnight walk
      through a wasteland

Mist that smothers us, spreads through the
      gaps between us

Everything stifles
Everything stifled.

A fire station appears
      Ship over the horizon

Subdued beeping, solemn
      like that cat's meow

Battleship skulks away,
      to a fire that isn't ours.

We stand in shock at what we have seen.
Reflect on this dystopian view

IS NOW A GOOD TIME?

This morning I woke up to 8:20's frown
 to find the clock face turned away from me.
Time is no longer on my side.

I've had many times before:
train times, tea times, times of wine and times of none,
but I never had the time to think about them.

Never mind running out of time,
 it's time who's running out on me.
I am timeless,

Like most of my desperate generation.

CANDLE

On your eighteenth birthday I cried all day
In the evening I dressed as a cat,
drank beer and did things I would never tell you

What would make you most happy?
That I cried all day for you?
Or that I'm making your mistakes for you?

"Mum, who's missing?"
Glancing at the middle seat in the car
Glancing at the fourth chair at the table

She kept finding 18-shaped confetti on the floor
in the weeks before, convinced it's you
the candle burning in the kitchen.

Baby footprints in milk,
pride of place photo album 1995

Baby coffin carpet burn,
pride of place first memory

WHAT'S THIS?

I don't really believe a candle is a person,
nor do I think this one is speaking to me.
It's crackling, more like a wireless.
I'm probably getting the wrong message anyway.

I've just thought about
all the things I could cry about,
but really I'm happy.

The wine bottle casts its five o'clock shadow
across the page, more dark than light.
If it were me I'd be so lonely.

ECHO

A cigarette won't keep me warm,
but neither will your breath.
Our laughter purples in the air
so we fill our speech marks with nothing.

You don't seem to mind
how the wind shakes me

CHANGED

I am about to know something.

That lazy Sunday morning ignorance,
the lazy ennui of not finding the time
to check a lottery ticket.

Life has changed without me

NONNET

Every night we watched the stars, bad times
made good. For this was the age of
starry skies, not a day
went by without my awe
of the clouds. Painted
we were but this
is just the
way things
end.

A VIEW

This is just another poem
about church spires
spearing through the guts
of supermarket car parks
as autumn starts to fall.
Some things change,
some things don't.

ETERNAL FLAME

There is always fire in the frost
Early morning heat,
to warm you
Something over the horizon,
to warn you

AWAY

every time
i fall asleep
it's like i'm on
a little ship

11th December, 1982. 11th December, 2012. Instead of the world ending we'll go back to the beginning. We could die tonight. If I died tonight I'd be happy. The 80s reminds me of Christmas. Photos of family 80s Christmases. Smoking indoors. Warm furniture. Homesick. Tonight I am my mother. Time for the time travel. Set the alarm for every 30 minutes the k-down to 1982. We're indestructible.

It's happened. I knew I was going to die tonight. It's my stalker, you see. He took tonight to decide to hunt me back to 1982. I do my best tragedy mask every time I check my phone.

Remember, he said. I have to buy my ticket first. He turns and asks the ballerina to play the part of the ticket-seller. You are a ballerina, I whisper to her. Now there are two actors. The bizarre love triangle. You proved it when you chose the same song. Partners in time.

I feel so extra-ordinary. The floor moves as we begin our journey. Make sure we leave on time. You look like a tragicomedy. I love you. Open your heart?

The mirror phase. I am the clown. Metropolis. The room gradually fades into black and white. Remember our parts. She looks at herself and witnesses her death in another universe. Anachronisms. The room is the club and we are the young hedonists. Make room for the bongo solo.

Missed calls aren't important when you're in the 80s, which explains the voicemails. Watchmen. I feel like I never should. Paranoia begins. One of us will die tonight. This is all part of the melodrama. I whisper hurried words for you to remember me by.

We can't buy drinks on card because we're too early. We did something wrong. I wouldn't buy a gin & tonic anyway. Because of us they stayed trapped in 1982. But they still aged. Time-travel wafts around us as we move around the crowd. They don't see us.

This is my punishment. It's a sin. I pray as they play. I pray because I'm losing my religion. Biblical light surrounds me. You're spiritual, she says, hand warily on my shoulder. Time's running out. This could be like Cinderella. If we get back in time the club may still be open. It's not. We find pizza in an abandoned car so we must be back in 2012. Take the tusk of the elephant. Experiment.

She explodes. It's the time travel, I said. Something went wrong. Blood. Who will die first? I want us to stay together in case we all die. Poetry on fire. We'll be the new Romantics. By now, so many pacts have been made that I no longer rely on myself.

It is hard to walk in the ice. Every tree hides a poet. Repeat the list after me. Don't leave me. Don't forget. Though we began together, we must end alone. We will all die tonight. I sleep, carefully.

LESS

"Excuse me, is this Good Hope?"
I hope not, but then I've long suspected
that I'm in the wrong place anyway.

I went to sleep upside down
to see if it would reverse things.
I woke up and everything was still all right.

I got up, pushed a hat on
like a ghost with a severed head
trying to prove it's still alive.

CIRCLING

You are here at 4am
to write depressing poetry.

You look old.

Well, you say. Well.
And I can't reply.

It's you with no emotion,
you announce in that tone of irretrievable loss.

I won't let your eyes pierce me.

Sinking ships and all that.

CIRCLING (ALTERNATE VERSION)

4am
here you are writing poems for me
to yourself.
I sigh
I can't say anything.

I'm the one with no emotion
not you.

That tone of irretrievable loss appears,

but nothing says "I need you"
like a 4am poem.

BAD NEWS

In the moment's silence before the 10 o'clock news,
there is the horror of childhood
staying up too late
hearing the troubles of the world.

Once you reach the end,
you can never see the beginning.

3AM

This is the time of stray cats and milk floats
Of shops humming their emptiness to nothing
Of rain, secret rain, generously saved
For when there's no-one to fall on

SOMETHING HE MIGHT SAY

"As for me, I like to keep all hours.
Except for 5pm –
that was always an awkward one"

CAFE CONVERSATION

You must have said something, I know.
I heard sentences. Or compliments.
I heard plates, crashing.

Someone buy a coffee. We need its presence.
Everything is charged these days:
The table, the air, this conversation.

The changes swing from this full stop.

SCHOLARS IN SQUALOR

Read between the lines,
there may be a poem here

SPEAK AGAIN

There is too much to say
about a plastic bag attempting suicide.

The breeze will always catch it
but even ghosts need to drift

THE MAY BUG

I hide from the breeze that can drown me,
overwhelm me with too much life
as I try to sail on to somewhere

No-one bought me flowers but they always show up,
and I could choke on their water
for the line between living and dying is the throat

A heroic may bug was crushed on the road,
so I too walk by the cars to prove I'm alive
and they miss me every time

GLASTONBURY

Where did we come from?
to this temporary city, to live the pop-up life of the outlaw,
    to be inside these electric city walls, to be outside the law,
    to be on the outskirts of life,
you see I came to look for answers and went round in
    circles, circles of stone, stones that roll, beaten by every
    element until I was in mine, the colours, the confusion,
    oh-the-people,
where sinners are mistaken for saints, where the journey
    must be made with candles, where the fire does not burn
    you, where there is life
and no time
no time at all

CONVERSATIONS WITH THE SKY

If only I could tell you how much
"I love the sky"
and tell you how I only love
what I cannot touch

Pantheon perfection,
the never-ending dome
ever-present reflection of us
like when a French girl
stands by a river and says
"I am feeling blue"
so looks upwards
or when my sister says
"Look how blue the sky is
I keep forgetting"
sees clouds gentler than the word
"thou"
new angels and white feathers
or veins of planes on the sky's pink face
or a sky that bursts into tears
sporadically
like one remembering grief and
swimming in it.

Ask the clouds what's coming,
they will always say
"rain".

4TH FEBRUARY

The green cloud hangs around me
the smoky ghost follows me

If he kisses her after I wake,
is it still night?

Listen
    The open secret will close

AMBULANCE OR NO AMBULANCE

each time a car comes, take it in turn to guess. ambulance, no ambulance or red car. if their guess comes, they get a point. if no-one has guessed ambulance and one comes, the game ends. number of ambulances seen determines the length of game. whoever guesses final ambulance wins. if neither guesses ambulance, the one with the highest points wins. if the points are a draw, sudden death: only guess ambulance or red car, eventually one will come and the guesser wins. (ties continue on). quick version for earlier in the night: groups of cars. Double ambulance followed by double red car: the game is over for good

Don't try to stop the ambulance.

geriatric. why did i write that word? the words, it seems are far from me.

you or i

it's a sign the food was not delivered. this endurance must last.

devil's causeway ..."callum"

why did i exchange 'giant' for 'devil'?

why make a mockery of the world to praise? why not show the world for its true, wonderful beauty?

if i ever saw a truly fantastic night i would be too overcome by its existence. such is England.

BEFORE THE CRASH

tell him about eaton cottage
is that all there is to tell
sadly, yes

I am travelling back in this poem
put this in your anthology
wow how postmodern, "she said".
Punctuation arrived, along with clarity.

I forgot, I was happy
The Page! The page!
"Pronounce your name like Katie first"

remember the essay
use more question marks

we are nothing like the Victorians
"What I don't like about Rothko is it's not very human"
the Rothko poems

WHAT DID WE WANT TO WRITE ABOUT?

what did we want to write about? is the train too far a strict

this is not going well. I am afraid. Utopia will only come if
you let it in. Poor John Barleycorn, cropredy

two stones grind to dust

all of this – cannot be happening. swan about teary eyed
bleary eyed denying everything but the light

the coca trees were swaying in their peculiar cardboard way.
It was a happier time, or so we thought

11:42

days lengthening ahead of me

days shrinking before me

night falls further than usual

everything that stands the end. is this the end? is there an end? we know there is no beginning. where was that moment, the turning-point? what was the point of no return? or have these lines always been here? the summer's rain, the winter's glare. fainting in spring and crashing in autumn.

why the lines changed without me knowing. that's how dreadful it was. figures of eight around me. remind myself to ask if i am a natural poet. doesn't make for happy people. desperately drinking to save our lives. a door, a window, anything would help right now. how does it work. how will i wake tomorrow. it was the tragedy you see. find something, quick

11:42 means 24th November – yesterday. That's when it happened, this is the meaning of the end. if only i could remember how happy i am. the unseeable future, the wholly other. how metafictional can things get without completely imploding. drowning; maybe it was may. oddities. weekends are where things don't happen, this terrifies me! technology is not my friend. oh, for a simpler life. moon slashed directly in half.

THE TIME TRAVELLER'S NOTE

Meet me in 1997.
It must be the past – the future does not exist.

It will be one of those days
filled with rain and slugs
creeping into your home, your life.

There comes a moment every evening
the sun sets
and the evening ennui rises.

When this moment comes
and you consider turning on the lights
then will I appear.

PRELUDE

The flux of clouds
that leak from my mind
like the tap's uncertain drip
flood the sky with grief
and echo against the weather.

Listen. Even ghosts need to drift.

A NIGHT FOR STRANGERS

Night falls, further than usual.

An army of Chinese lanterns
constellates above you.

Streetlights are brighter than the moon.
Step on neighbourhood leaves.

A shaky glance down the alley:
a frog looks back.

Walk into tomorrow's cobwebs;
thank the car that almost hit you.

headlights like a sun that rose for you alone,
looked you over: all that will be, all that won't be.

A bin man's demonic laughter

POEM FOR A GOOD MOOD

Streetlights have minds of their own around here,
so I turn to the stars for guidance.

In the dormant volcano of my evergreen,
ever-growing memory,

death appears dancing with a cigarette.
Hollow eyes. Lacy dress.

Why do I sit here looking only for sunlight
when I could be hidden, cradled in

the hand of some heavenly giant?
(I was dreaming, I was happy)

Live for a living
Harness the sky

HEAVEN ON EARTH

On days when the washing machine
drowns out your thoughts

When people play piano
to the muted beat of raindrops

When jewelled saints
appear in your dreams

When the sky is absent
and life must be present:

Where is heaven if not here?

UNNATURE

All is natural
but the traffic cone in the water
interrupting the peace
with an urban beauty

Like vapour trails,
the heavenly lines linking
mackerel clouds and feathers:
trains of thought

Like the tracks,
the veins on England's skin
travelling to the heart,
wherever that may be

FRIDAY 13TH

Oh, vicious lights,
modern life,
sad decorations,
plastic happiness.

Teens roll fags.
(Nothing can hide their boredom.)
Static plays on the radio,
no one knows.

Every face a blank,
every voice a drone.
Everyone's a winner.

The forlorn sky weeps,
sporadically,
for the missing sun

WEST

We rode towards the edge:
a horizon so perfect,
it must have been fictional.
The sun
like a penny that hadn't yet dropped

A DAILY WAR

The West takes the sun from us
and sets fire to the sky

Leaves us with starry embers
to ponder through the night

SYMPHONY IN BLACK

I pale against the shadow
of the shattering night

And like an empty ink pen
remembering the words it once wrote

I remember the fine light of day,
the promise of the horizon.

IF ONLY

The finite grace
of the sunset

The darkening
of shadowy clouds

The gradual onset
of cold

The terrible truth
in understanding

That you don't know what I mean.

POST SCRIPT

This poem protects
the gaze on the train tracks,
the vacant sky
the fearful thought.

(Too close)

Is this a new verse
or the end of the line?

SAY SOMETHING

Awake and cross yourself
at the thought of the day
of the magpies lying in wait

Assemble the morning
like flat-pack furniture
blurred skies

The rain is up
the phone lines are down
(one for sorrow)

WEATHER, 8AM

Lingering mist. Light rainfall.

Awake in a cloud,
heavy with last night.
Regrets fly around,
mingling with dreams
and half-truths.

INTERLUDE

Skyclad,
I worship.

You,
I,
and the sky

SCENES

i
Stepping along the tallest bridge
in early-morning Bern:
our silent arguments hanging in the air
with the mist

ii
Black and white night
in the endless maize fields:
I follow you and the traitorous moon
into a Lincolnshire jungle

iii
You and I share
one final fragile moment
at the frontier of day and night
Sleeping swans on the lake

THE CATASTROPHE

The ground pulls the rain from the clouds
you didn't leave, you were pushed

A man made of wine ferments in his suit
"just look what you've done to me"

Spider plants crawl around half alive
spiky resentment that never dies

How can the world stand so much rain?
how can the sky carry it?

CITY EYES

I tread streets my mother never dreamed of:
far from the eyes of my past,
sugar rain wraps me in cold asylum.
The claddagh ring points north.

The ladder against the fence blesses me
as I stumble towards the end of my life.
Tired houses comfort each other,
terraced brotherhood in bricks.

The city, forlorn and restless,
reflects in my eyes
and finds peace in the art above,
scanning the skies for the future

The country is not mine
but this street belongs to me

A LONE DREAM

The pylons ruin my view
but complete it;
black wires crossing my sky
with too much life.

I lie here and mourn
our imagined future
until you reach into me,
hook me from sleep.

CURL UP

I come to you,
curl up against the tyranny of the storm
hide from the sky's angry face
hear sorrows drown themselves
forget that for hundreds of tears

I have stood,
the lonely tower above the mist,
the statue beaten by weather,
the lighthouse without beacon.

Rain ends.
The door awaits.

CHANGES

You walk in:
face a blank sky,
empty of meaning

An aura of cold air clings to you;
the idea of winter
creeping into the room
as an afterthought

And look at us:
two stone pillars of sadness
waiting for the other to speak

GONE

The cuckoo talks of cowardice
as I dream of single magpies.
Hopeless advice in a foreign language
keeps me awake at 4.23am.

Now is the time for
casual *hi*'s, 6am goodbyes,
the morning party, the leaving train:
delayed
(but not enough).

An aeroplane cries across the sky
A tree sings an invisible song
Milk floats slip by in the darkness
following you like a hearse

FAILURE

"There is no tragedy like this under the sky"

The pen weighs down my hand,
these words grow far away from me.

But the skies call me on a purple Thursday
(as they always do),
illuminate the pylons
marching across the earth like prisoners,
the tortured giants
of an electrical war.

Nautical clouds sail above
oblivious to pain
dragging their hulls on our seabed
the wrecking, the wrecked

Silence. All is gone.
I am alone once more,

I have written this poem so many times
and the title is always 'failure'.

LIGHTNESS

I wake to find unhappiness on my skin
(yours or mine, I wonder)

I turn on the light and the bulb explodes
reminds me that all ideas can be monsters

An implausible lilac shines through
the window that never shuts

I won't close my eyes
if the stars are out.

PARK BENCH, 4PM

A day when everything looks clear.
Lines sharp. Boundaries defined.

Even the air is clear,
until I smoke it.
Whispers and ghosts appear, challenging
the clarity of day.

A grey cloud sets in my peripheral vision.

INSTINCT

To look,
after you.

You walk on,
I watch from behind,

forever looking after you.

NEW GIRL

Looking just like my grandmother did,
eyes above the camera,
perfect curls and pearls
tapping on the frame
like typewritten poems
or ghostly steps on a staircase

A JUICE ODYSSEY

Nothing but pineapples
fall out of your mouth,
choking the both of us.
Tropical lies. Punctured lungs.
A favourite wound opened up.

SIGNS

Seven spotted ladybirds fly
into the future. Scattered.
Lie sleeping with knives
to fend off the love.

A half-eaten apple smirks
a rusty grin at me.
Sunflowers always look east.
A bouquet of faces.

THE UNSETTLEMENT

Memory is that way we know
that leads to the green heart's field.
My childhood paved with cola bottles.
Yours with fresh apples.

I follow your train of thought,
stopping with each breath.
(Who goes there?)

I look for your queen and find ten:
your number one
and me, the cipher next door.

You glance to me and see
two years' worth of dreams in my look.
Take them, and slip away
very much noticed.

The one that got away.
The dream unremembered.

NOOSED

You dived for pearls
in her bottomless eyes;
I strung them round my neck
and was silenced.

Chained to the letter D,
I followed your lead,
catching the shards of oyster
that never broke my heart.

I was not your ocean,
but you were not my rope.

CLARITY

A day when everything looks clear.
Lines defined. Boundaries defined.

Even the air is clear, until I smoke it.
Whispers and ghosts arise, challenging
one moment of peace.

A grey cloud sets in my peripheral vision.

POEM FOR THE DAMNED

A juice odyssey
a day's reverie
a smoky memory

an end to misery
Amsterdamned trickery
what is this hooker

NO CAMP WITHOUT FIRE

We three trees sit by the swamp,
bothered only by gnats and our troubles.

This is what they mean when they say
the woods are singing.

Moon totters above split end branches.
Words spill out and condensate,
mingling with fog until
the dots of my i's become distant stars
and my harshest k's are bats.

The fucker burnt my upholstery.

POEM FOR A PENCIL

Yes, there is one thing
I'll never tell you,
and that's 'the truth'.

The cries from next door
crack open our silence
but our best words are
said with the eyes.

Unseen, the Artex waves of the sky
crash above us, filling up
this bedroom with blue notes.

Hookers smoke Vogue cigarettes.
Which is true,
but you'll never believe me.

ST PATRICK'S DAY

Went to Wetherspooons
to spend twenty quid on an argument.

Green eyes become black
as blood becomes whiskey.
            (For the love of Christ)

Despair tastes like garden peas,
desertion like pain au chocolat,
and absinthe makes the heart grow
thinner.
Persona non grata.

THE FROG

The first time we saw the frog
we were high. We named an alley for it,
marking the spot in the memories
we mapped with our hands.

The second time we saw the frog
we were down, needing the
frog's affirmation. We helped it
on its way, hoping for good things.

The third time I saw the frog
I was alone. Another couple in our position.
Don't touch, she says. I was only
trying to help, says he.

The final time we saw the frog
it was dead. Brains out for the lads,
mistaken for the leaf
it always wanted to be.

UNTITLED

I lift up my left arm
to see chicken pox scars
raise like rain drops on my shoulder

A bloody sunset
comes to warn me
red-eyed and struggling
like a coke can
trying to sail across the river

This is still not a poem about you.

SAINT BONFIRE

She sings with her gaze up
finding notes in the air.

Remember when I was afraid
of that smoke alarm
The saintly eye watching the fire

Grey on grey
smoke rises to meet its maker

We watch by the water
safe as the house's reflection.

(Wait
Where did the evening go?)

MORIRE

"I fell as bodies fall, for dead"

A blackbird pecks another blackbird
to death – over strawberries. A woman's
skeleton watches TV for three years
unnoticed. Barrels of laughs are pushed
over waterfalls. A bowl of freshly
washed plums topple into Hell.
A cigarette thrown from the 39th
floor lands on a pigeon. Death
and gravity are one and the same.

PROFESSIONAL PEDESTRIAN

Walking east to escape the afternoon,
I find on my path
twenty-one pennies
to reward my twenty-one years
of service to the ground.

Traveller's limbo; the prize
for most professional pedestrian.
The ever-revolving front door changes
in the squall.
                    Where am I

APFELSAFT

It began with a Queen wasp
awaking from her winter sleep:
it was the day after I realised
those mystic birds that seemed

to follow me everywhere were
in fact only sparrows.
When I heard the news, I slumped
like a willow.

Folk music sounds like flowers. I listened
to Her Majesty's buzz and compared
my bra to a pair of hanging baskets.
Stumbled across some apple

worshippers. When I write my novel
I will devote a whole chapter
to apple juice. I'm more of a passion
fruit girl, but I caved in like

an old raspberry and joined them.

SYNAESTHESIA KALEIDOSCOPE

Remember

"the cinematographer's party"
(where I finally cracked your lying face)

I saw shattered sunsets
and the constellations of the bar
speaking spirits swimming in Coke

voices
            floating   you are Paul Simon
carousel

NURSE THE BOTTLE

Nurse the bottle, not the baby. This is the meaning of those dreams, dreams of marriage and children. All they mean is terrible things to come. Strangers, perhaps that is what I need. Haunting songs, filling me up with memory, sun-drenched smiles that only exist in the past. Oh I wish you were with me, the Well-Beloved. Flit into someone else so I can carry on. Entrapment of the spirit, that is what it was once called. If only the spirit would touch me again, just once. One of those nights again. What have I done to my destroyed self. If everyone knew the truth about everything. Would there be any more meaning? "What goes around comes around" but it has been going round for far too long. How low can I slip, I wonder? What horrors await me.

I WALK

I walk, cloaked like Mary. Rain washes down, smearing my glasses and dampening my shoulders. Purgatorio, another pilgrim turns as I do, with a semi adequate umbrella. We climb in tandem, the steepness lightening as we come to our destination

the beatific vision

the cleansing rain

glory hallelujah

pretty little baby

CLAY PIGEON

Shooting for the moon
straying into day, stealing from the sun

Shooting the winter haze
creeping through bones and woodland

Shooting away the hangovers
and with them the dreams

Cats and combine harvesters pass me by

the moon held up by a tree
shooting at the moon
the streets the colour of winter
the wintry haze over the wood

SHADY GROVES

I sought solace amongst no one,
friends in the darkness.
Who is to say what can happen
when there is no witness

Mutineers flood the streets
drowned in puddles crushed by feet,
bare-bone branches lost their crew
of gold-brown-yellow coloured hue,
the captain thinks and smokes his pipe
this tree and I, we are alike.
"I'm the ship you sail, the boards you walk",
said the tree to the man, if the tree could talk.

UNTITLED

Listen to mother's Joni Mitchell albums
Sneak out to the beacon of hope
The corner shop,
the drunks getting drunker,
the lonely buying crisps
the hopeless scratching cards with coins
Comfort in neon
I don't want the world today.

UNTITLED

You nod, and we all understand.
You trip and we fall.
You speak balloon animals (words) and we wrestle them to
the ground

Loneliness is leaving a candle burning
Whilst you sleep the day away

Lightning Source UK Ltd.
Milton Keynes UK
UKHW02f0610120218
317732UK00004BA/163/P